Basic Skills and Beyond
Addition & Subtraction
Grades 2–3
by Bill Linderman

Activities Support These Learning Outcomes

Number Sense and Operations
- Understand place value, equivalencies, and representations of whole numbers
- Understand the meanings and properties of operations
- Develop strategies for accurate methods of computation and estimation

Algebra
- Express quantities and relationships using letters, symbols, and equations

Carson-Dellosa Publishing Company, Inc.
Greensboro, North Carolina

Credits

Addition & Subtraction Grades 2-3

Editor:
Amy Gamble

Layout Design and Art Coordination:
Jon Nawrocik

Inside Illustrations:
Mike Dammer

Cover Design:
Peggy Jackson

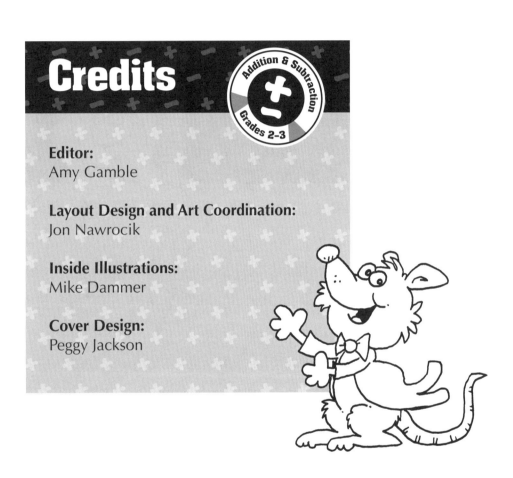

ISBN 0-88724-189-1

Table of Contents

Introduction

Mathematics is an exciting subject! With some practice and determination, learning math skills like addition and subtraction can be very rewarding. This book will add to your students' love of learning and will give them the opportunity to practice and have fun with the addition and subtraction skills they learn in the second and third grades.

This book is meant to catch students' attention with interesting and exciting math activities that draw them to the application process. It is this practical involvement that allows students to enhance their mathematics abilities. As the basic skills are mastered, these operations become a natural part of their every day lives. A joy begins to grow inside the heart of the child learning math. When joy is present, the sky is the limit!

Here are a few suggestions to optimize the time spent practicing the skills from this book:

A. Make sure that all math is introduced using hands-on manipulatives! After all, numbers are just symbols. The child must associate these symbols with real objects and quantities in their world. Buttons, pennies, grapes, etc., are excellent manipulatives to use to extend the addition and subtraction practice pages of this book.

B. Glue white paper to the tops of jar lids. Write a two-digit number on each lid, such as 24, 31, etc. Have the child pick two lids and add the numbers together. As students mix and match to make new problems, encourage them to notice patterns.

C. Add prices to small toys. Ask the children to find two toys that come closest to equaling one dollar. Or, let them pick out small toys from the store and use these for playing this addition game.

D. Practice measuring using centimeters. Find small objects in your house or classroom that have lengths of 9 or less centimeters. Have the child pick two items, measure their lengths in centimeters, and add the measurements together.

E. Find numbers in the real world and have students list all of the addends that can be added together to equal that amount. For example, if the child is 7 or 8, have them discover all of the addends that equal these amounts. Then, they can go to their brother's or sister's ages, their mom's and dad's ages, their street addresses, the number of houses on their blocks, etc.

F. Take fact families from pages in this book and write them on flash cards. Have students play school and practice learning these facts.

G. As children are first introduced to pictographs, have them make their own graphs. They can ask friends and neighbors their favorite colors. Assist your child in creating these graphs. Ask addition and subtraction questions about the graph when it is complete.

Name _____ Date _____

A Symbol of Addition

Directions: Add. Use the answers to color each shape according to the code below.

Code

6 = yellow   9 = blue   8 = red   7 = green   10 = red

5 + 1	4 + 4	2 + 7
0 + 7 3 + 4		4 + 5
4 + 2	5 + 5	3 + 3
6 + 2	3 + 7	5 + 3
	10 + 0	8 + 0	6 + 4
8 + 1	7 + 1	5 + 1
9 + 0 3 + 6	2 + 8	0 + 7 2 + 5 6 + 1

Name _____ Date _____

Something Is Missing

Directions: Fill in the missing addends along the path. Go back and add details to the snowman at the start to make him match the snowman at the finish.

Example

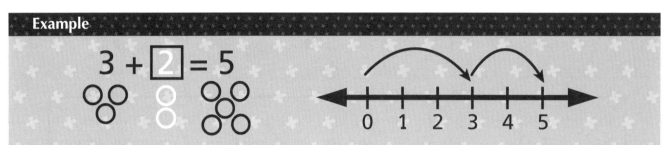

$$3 + \boxed{2} = 5$$

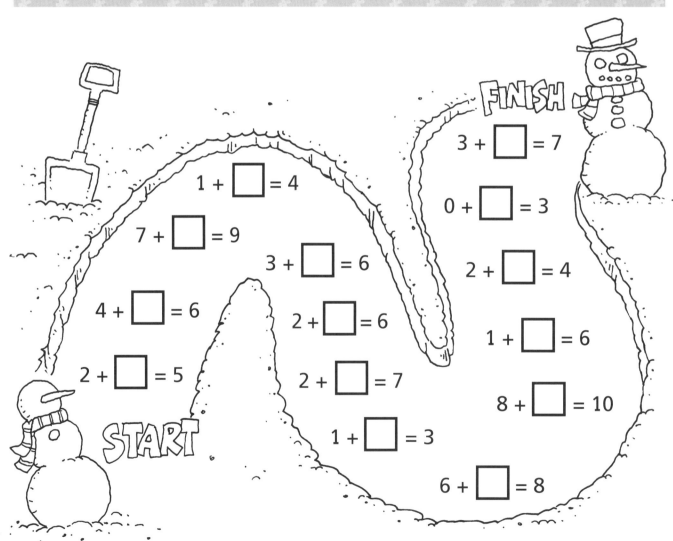

$$1 + \square = 4$$

$$7 + \square = 9$$

$$4 + \square = 6$$

$$2 + \square = 5$$

$$3 + \square = 6$$

$$2 + \square = 6$$

$$2 + \square = 7$$

$$1 + \square = 3$$

$$3 + \square = 7$$

$$0 + \square = 3$$

$$2 + \square = 4$$

$$1 + \square = 6$$

$$8 + \square = 10$$

$$6 + \square = 8$$

START

FINISH

Rodeo Roper!

Directions: Add. Rope together problems with matching sums.

Example

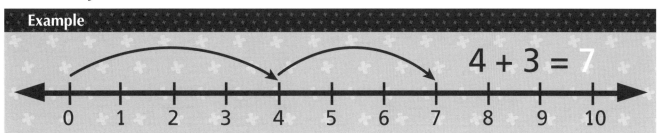

$$4 + 3 = 7$$

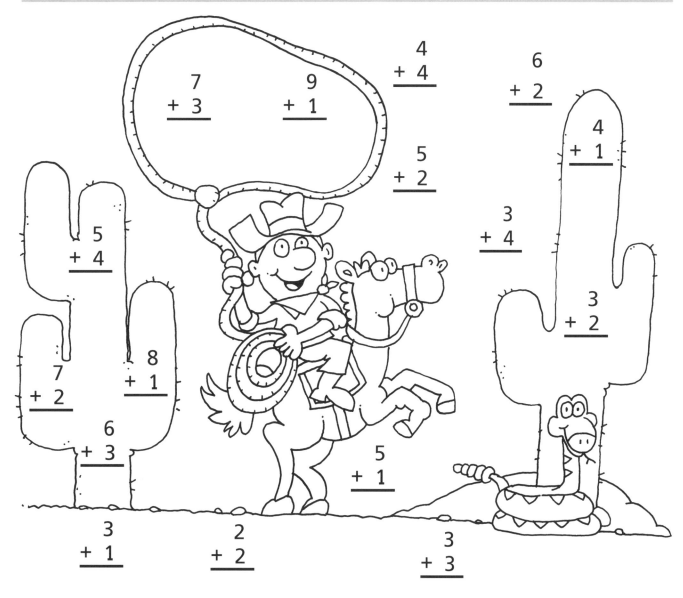

$$\begin{array}{r} 7 \\ + 3 \\ \hline \end{array} \qquad \begin{array}{r} 9 \\ + 1 \\ \hline \end{array} \qquad \begin{array}{r} 4 \\ + 4 \\ \hline \end{array} \qquad \begin{array}{r} 6 \\ + 2 \\ \hline \end{array}$$

$$\begin{array}{r} 5 \\ + 2 \\ \hline \end{array} \qquad \begin{array}{r} 4 \\ + 1 \\ \hline \end{array}$$

$$\begin{array}{r} 5 \\ + 4 \\ \hline \end{array} \qquad \begin{array}{r} 3 \\ + 4 \\ \hline \end{array}$$

$$\begin{array}{r} 7 \\ + 2 \\ \hline \end{array} \qquad \begin{array}{r} 8 \\ + 1 \\ \hline \end{array} \qquad \begin{array}{r} 3 \\ + 2 \\ \hline \end{array}$$

$$\begin{array}{r} 6 \\ + 3 \\ \hline \end{array}$$

$$\begin{array}{r} 5 \\ + 1 \\ \hline \end{array}$$

$$\begin{array}{r} 3 \\ + 1 \\ \hline \end{array} \qquad \begin{array}{r} 2 \\ + 2 \\ \hline \end{array} \qquad \begin{array}{r} 3 \\ + 3 \\ \hline \end{array}$$

Diamond Mine

Directions: Add. Use a ruler to draw lines connecting like sums. How many diamonds can you find?

8 + 2 = _____ ●

3 + 3 = _____ ●   ● 2 + 3 = _____

4 + 5 = _____ ●   ● 2 + 5 = _____

7 + 5 = _____ ●   ● 3 + 1 = _____

1 + 7 = _____ ●   ● 5 + 6 = _____

$$\begin{array}{r} 6 \\ +\ 4 \\ \hline \end{array}$$ ●   ● $$\begin{array}{r} 5 \\ +\ 5 \\ \hline \end{array}$$

1 + 4 = _____ ●   ● 2 + 4 = _____

3 + 4 = _____ ●   ● 6 + 3 = _____

2 + 2 = _____ ●   ● 3 + 9 = _____

8 + 3 = _____ ●   ● 4 + 4 = _____

● 7 + 3 = _____

Name _____ Date _____

White Water Challenge

Directions: Add. Then, using the key, match each sum with a letter to see what you're doing when you take on each new challenge in math.

START 4 + 2 =   5 + 4 =   6 + 6 =   8 + 5 =   3 + 4 =   5 + 7 =   9 + 6 =   8 + 3 =

8 + 6 =   9 + 3 =   7 + 4 =   9 + 5 =   7 + 3 =   3 + 1 =

8 + 4 =   7 + 8 =   6 + 7 =   4 + 4 =   2 + 3 =   7 + 7 =

YOU MADE IT!

| 4 = R | 10 = E | 5 = T | 11 = G | 6 = C | 12 = I |
| 7 = B | 13 = M | 8 = A | 14 = H | 9 = L | 15 = N |

Polygon Pile

Directions: Add. Color the shapes with even sums yellow and the shapes with odd sums blue.

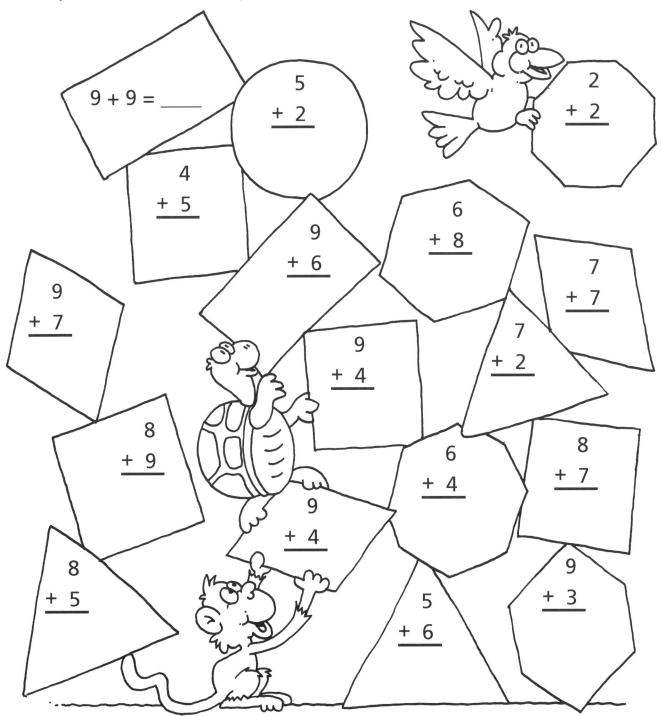

$9 + 9 =$ _____

$\begin{array}{r} 5 \\ + 2 \\ \hline \end{array}$

$\begin{array}{r} 2 \\ + 2 \\ \hline \end{array}$

$\begin{array}{r} 4 \\ + 5 \\ \hline \end{array}$

$\begin{array}{r} 9 \\ + 6 \\ \hline \end{array}$

$\begin{array}{r} 6 \\ + 8 \\ \hline \end{array}$

$\begin{array}{r} 7 \\ + 7 \\ \hline \end{array}$

$\begin{array}{r} 9 \\ + 7 \\ \hline \end{array}$

$\begin{array}{r} 9 \\ + 4 \\ \hline \end{array}$

$\begin{array}{r} 7 \\ + 2 \\ \hline \end{array}$

$\begin{array}{r} 8 \\ + 9 \\ \hline \end{array}$

$\begin{array}{r} 6 \\ + 4 \\ \hline \end{array}$

$\begin{array}{r} 8 \\ + 7 \\ \hline \end{array}$

$\begin{array}{r} 8 \\ + 5 \\ \hline \end{array}$

$\begin{array}{r} 9 \\ + 4 \\ \hline \end{array}$

$\begin{array}{r} 5 \\ + 6 \\ \hline \end{array}$

$\begin{array}{r} 9 \\ + 3 \\ \hline \end{array}$

Out of Order

Directions: Add. Match the problems with the same addends to create compound words.

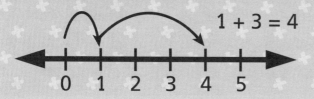 $1 + 3 = 4$

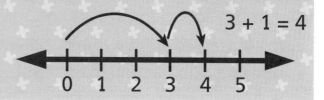 $3 + 1 = 4$

$4 + 5 =$ ____

lady_____

$7 + 6 =$ ____

gold_____

$4 + 7 =$ ____ (work)

$9 + 1 =$ ____ (bow)

$2 + 8 =$ ____ (box)

$8 + 9 =$ ____ (tail)

$8 + 5 =$ ____

butter_____

$9 + 8 =$ ____

pony_____

$5 + 4 =$ ____ (bug)

$6 + 7 =$ ____ (fish)

$5 + 3 =$ ____

birth_____

$2 + 3 =$ ____

side_____

$3 + 5 =$ ____ (day)

$3 + 2 =$ ____ (walk)

$7 + 4 =$ ____

home_____

$8 + 2 =$ ____

sand_____

$4 + 9 =$ ____ (plane)

$5 + 8 =$ ____ (fly)

$1 + 9 =$ ____

rain_____

$9 + 4 =$ ____

air_____

Bravo for Zero!

Directions: On each mountain, write the number that is lost when you go through the tunnel.

A number added to zero always equals that number. $8 + 0 = \underline{8}$

Zero subtracted from a number always equals that number. $3 - 0 = \underline{3}$

A number subtracted from itself always equals zero. $2 - 2 = \underline{0}$

Three Tree

Column Addition 1-9

Directions: Add.

$$
\begin{array}{r} 3 \\ 7 \\ +\ 4 \\ \hline \end{array}
$$

$$
\begin{array}{r} 3 \\ 6 \\ +\ 3 \\ \hline \end{array}
$$

$$
\begin{array}{r} 7 \\ 6 \\ +\ 2 \\ \hline \end{array}
$$

$$
\begin{array}{r} 6 \\ 3 \\ +\ 5 \\ \hline \end{array}
$$

$$
\begin{array}{r} 4 \\ 8 \\ +\ 2 \\ \hline \end{array}
$$

$$
\begin{array}{r} 3 \\ 5 \\ +\ 2 \\ \hline \end{array}
$$

$$
\begin{array}{r} 7 \\ 2 \\ +\ 4 \\ \hline \end{array}
$$

$$
\begin{array}{r} 4 \\ 5 \\ +\ 1 \\ \hline \end{array}
$$

$$
\begin{array}{r} 5 \\ 4 \\ +\ 3 \\ \hline \end{array}
$$

$$
\begin{array}{r} 1 \\ 8 \\ +\ 5 \\ \hline \end{array}
$$

$$
\begin{array}{r} 7 \\ 8 \\ +\ 1 \\ \hline \end{array}
$$

$$
\begin{array}{r} 2 \\ 5 \\ +\ 7 \\ \hline \end{array}
$$

$$
\begin{array}{r} 5 \\ 4 \\ +\ 6 \\ \hline \end{array}
$$

$$
\begin{array}{r} 5 \\ 9 \\ +\ 3 \\ \hline \end{array}
$$

$$
\begin{array}{r} 2 \\ 1 \\ +\ 4 \\ \hline \end{array}
$$

$$
\begin{array}{r} 2 \\ 4 \\ +\ 6 \\ \hline \end{array}
$$

Name _____ Date _____

Asteroid Roundup

Directions: Add.

Example

$(3 + 2) + 4 = $ _____
$5 \quad + 4 = \underline{9}$

Always add inside the parentheses first.

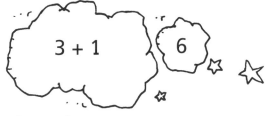

1. $(3 + 1) + 6 = $ _____

2. $(1 + 6) + 5 = $ _____

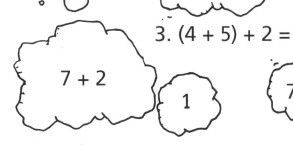

3. $(4 + 5) + 2 = $ _____

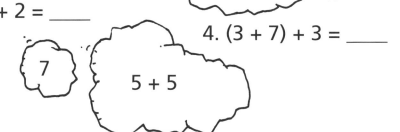

4. $(3 + 7) + 3 = $ _____

5. $(7 + 2) + 1 = $ _____

6. $7 + (5 + 5) = $ _____

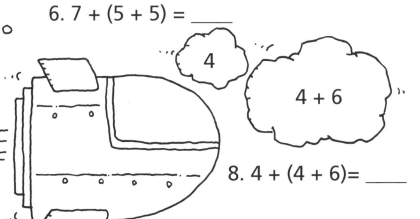

7. $3 + (4 + 2) = $ _____

8. $4 + (4 + 6) = $ _____

Name _____ Date _____

Perimeter Challenge

Directions: Write an equation to find the perimeter of each shape.

Example

To find the perimeter of a shape, add the lengths of the sides.

$1 + 2 + 2 = 5$
$P = 5$ cm

1.

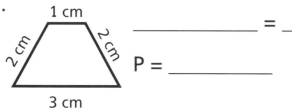

_____ = _____

P = _____

2.

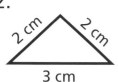

_____ = _____

P = _____

3.

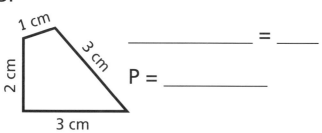

_____ = _____

P = _____

4.

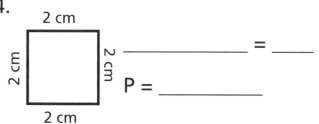

_____ = _____

P = _____

5.

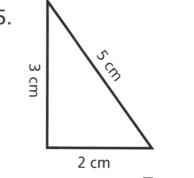

_____ = _____

P = _____

6.

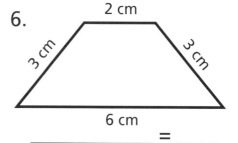

_____ = _____

P = _____

7.

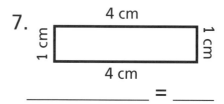

_____ = _____

P = _____

Name _____ Date _____

Measuring Adds Up

Directions: Measure each line with a centimeter ruler. Add the four lengths together.

1.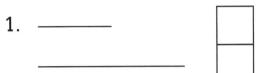

2.

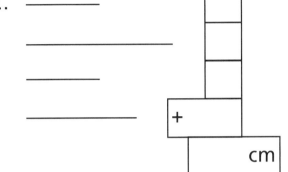

3.

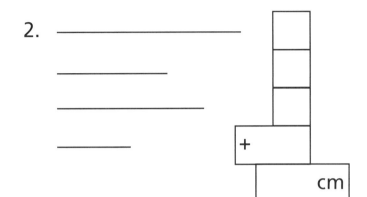

4.

5.

© Carson-Dellosa

Name _____ Date _____

Fly, Fly Away

Directions: Subtract. Color each bubble according to the key.

Key

1 = orange   2 = green   3 = yellow
4 = blue   5 = red   6 = purple

$$\begin{array}{r} 8 \\ -\ 5 \\ \hline \end{array}$$

$$\begin{array}{r} 3 \\ -\ 2 \\ \hline \end{array}$$

$$\begin{array}{r} 7 \\ -\ 4 \\ \hline \end{array}$$

$$\begin{array}{r} 10 \\ -\ 6 \\ \hline \end{array}$$

$$\begin{array}{r} 5 \\ -\ 3 \\ \hline \end{array}$$

$$\begin{array}{r} 9 \\ -\ 3 \\ \hline \end{array}$$

$$\begin{array}{r} 7 \\ -\ 5 \\ \hline \end{array}$$

$$\begin{array}{r} 9 \\ -\ 6 \\ \hline \end{array}$$

$$\begin{array}{r} 5 \\ -\ 1 \\ \hline \end{array}$$

$$\begin{array}{r} 10 \\ -\ 5 \\ \hline \end{array}$$

$$\begin{array}{r} 10 \\ -\ 7 \\ \hline \end{array}$$

$$\begin{array}{r} 6 \\ -\ 2 \\ \hline \end{array}$$

$$\begin{array}{r} 9 \\ -\ 4 \\ \hline \end{array}$$

$$\begin{array}{r} 4 \\ -\ 3 \\ \hline \end{array}$$

$$\begin{array}{r} 8 \\ -\ 3 \\ \hline \end{array}$$

Name _____ Date _____

Let's Compare!

Directions: Cross out the correct number of objects in each group. Subtract. Compare the differences.

Example

$6 - 2$ $\boxed{<}$ $7 - 2$

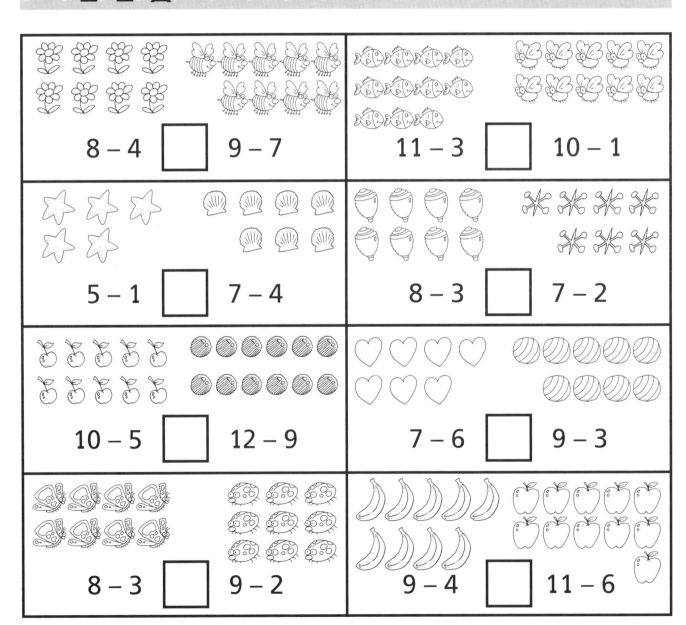

$8 - 4$ $\square$ $9 - 7$ $11 - 3$ $\square$ $10 - 1$

$5 - 1$ $\square$ $7 - 4$ $8 - 3$ $\square$ $7 - 2$

$10 - 5$ $\square$ $12 - 9$ $7 - 6$ $\square$ $9 - 3$

$8 - 3$ $\square$ $9 - 2$ $9 - 4$ $\square$ $11 - 6$

Subtraction, Ahoy!

Subtraction Facts to 12

Directions: Subtract. Write the answers in the puzzle in the form of words.

Across:

2. 8	4. 11	5. 12	7. 9	8. 7
− 2	− 3	− 5	− 3	− 4

9. 9	10. 10	11. 11	12. 8
− 4	− 6	− 4	− 5

Down:

1. 9	3. 12	5. 12
− 1	− 7	− 6

6. 12	7. 10
− 3	− 3

8. 9
− 7

9. 10	10. 6
− 5	− 2

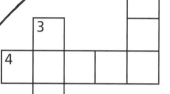

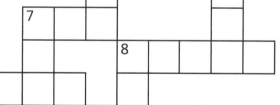

Name _____   Date _____

Frog Jumping Contest

Directions: Subtract. Each frog gets three jumps, only landing on his number. Which frog won the contest?

13	12	14	14	13	15	12
− 6	− 5	− 7	− 8	− 7	− 7	− 6

14	13	15	11	14	10	15
− 6	− 8	− 9	− 4	− 9	− 5	− 8

13	9	11	10	10	12	15
− 9	− 2	− 9	− 6	− 4	− 8	− 6

14	9	12	11	10	13	11
− 5	− 6	− 4	− 3	− 7	− 5	− 8

Name _____ Date _____

Fact Families

Directions: Add and subtract.

3, 9, 12

3 + 9 = _____

12 − 9 = _____

9 + 3 = _____

12 − 3 = _____

7, 8, 15

7 + 8 = _____

15 − 8 = _____

8 + 7 = _____

15 − 7 = _____

5, 9, 14

9 + 5 = _____

14 − 5 = _____

5 + 9 = _____

14 − 9 = _____

6, 7, 13

6 + 7 = _____

13 − 7 = _____

7 + 6 = _____

13 − 6 = _____

5, 6, 11

5 + 6 = _____

11 − 6 = _____

6 + 5 = _____

11 − 5 = _____

7, 9, 16

7 + 9 = _____

16 − 9 = _____

9 + 7 = _____

16 − 7 = _____

Name _____ Date _____

Animal Favorites

Directions: Use the tallies to fill in the bar
graph. Label the graph. Answer the questions.

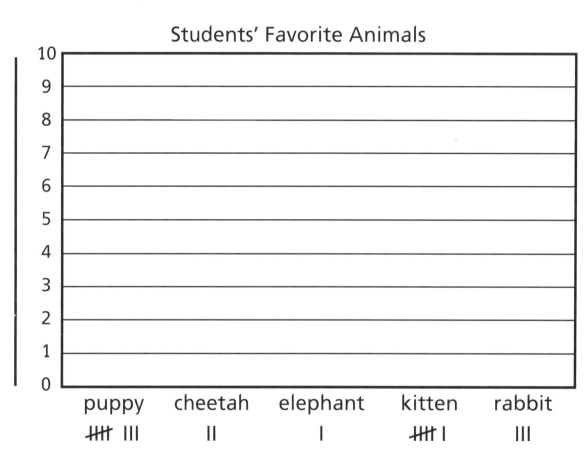

Students' Favorite Animals

	puppy	cheetah	elephant	kitten	rabbit
tallies	⳩⳩ III	II	I	⳩⳩ I	III

1. How many students chose puppies and kittens altogether? _____

2. How many more students picked cheetahs than elephants? _____

3. How many students voted in all? _____

4. What is the difference in votes between the least popular and
   most popular animal? _____

5. How many students chose rabbits or puppies? _____

Name _____ Date _____

Addition vs. Subtraction

Directions: Add and subtract. Then, compare using the symbols >, <, and =. Give Mr. Addition or Mr. Subtraction a point each time his answer is greater than the other. If the answers are equal, neither gets a point. Who won?

1. 3 + 4 ☐ 10 – 5

2. 2 + 5 ☐ 15 – 9

3. 3 + 8 ☐ 18 – 9

4. 4 + 0 ☐ 17 – 8

5. 3 + 2 ☐ 11 – 5

6. 2 + 7 ☐ 11 – 3

7. 1 + 3 ☐ 6 – 1

8. 3 + 5 ☐ 17 – 9

9. 2 + 2 ☐ 7 – 3

10. 4 + 2 ☐ 11 – 4

11. 5 + 1 ☐ 12 – 5

12. 8 + 9 ☐ 17 – 4

13. 3 + 3 ☐ 9 – 8

14. 4 + 8 ☐ 17 – 8

15. 7 + 5 ☐ 14 – 6

<u>Tally Results</u>

Mr. Addition:

Mr. Subtraction:

The Bigger Spender

Two-Digit Addition • No Regrouping

Directions: Add. Circle the greater amount.

Eva	Katelyn
34¢	23¢
+ 25¢	+ 52¢

David	Mark
53¢	14¢
+ 26¢	+ 53¢

Marlene	Gwen
36¢	21¢
+ 13¢	+ 23¢

Earl	Heather
50¢	30¢
+ 28¢	+ 49¢

Aaron	Natania
52¢	64¢
+ 17¢	+ 15¢

Aiko	Cheryl
44¢	23¢
+ 42¢	+ 52¢

Kanoa	Tabitha
38¢	25¢
+ 20¢	+ 32¢

Amy	Wolfgang
35¢	25¢
+ 11¢	+ 62¢

What to Say

Two-Digit Addition
No Regrouping

Directions: Add. Then, to find out what everyone likes to say when they're on TV, color each space yellow that is a digit in an answer below. Color all other spaces blue.

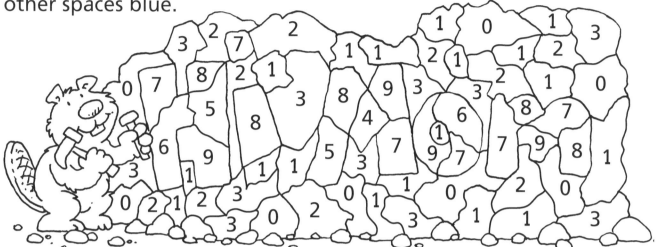

1. 42 + 36	2. 16 + 72	3. 45 + 13	4. 51 + 38	5. 38 + 41
6. 25 + 53	7. 62 + 13	8. 42 + 56	9. 37 + 22	10. 33 + 45
11. 48 + 31	12. 23 + 61	13. 60 + 38	14. 16 + 81	15. 51 + 36
16. 64 + 32	17. 41 + 38	18. 34 + 23	19. 37 + 41	20. 63 + 15

Name _____ Date _____

The Addition Road!

Two-Digit Addition
Regrouping

Directions: Guess which number is the missing addend. Add to check your guess. See how fast you can make it to the finish line!

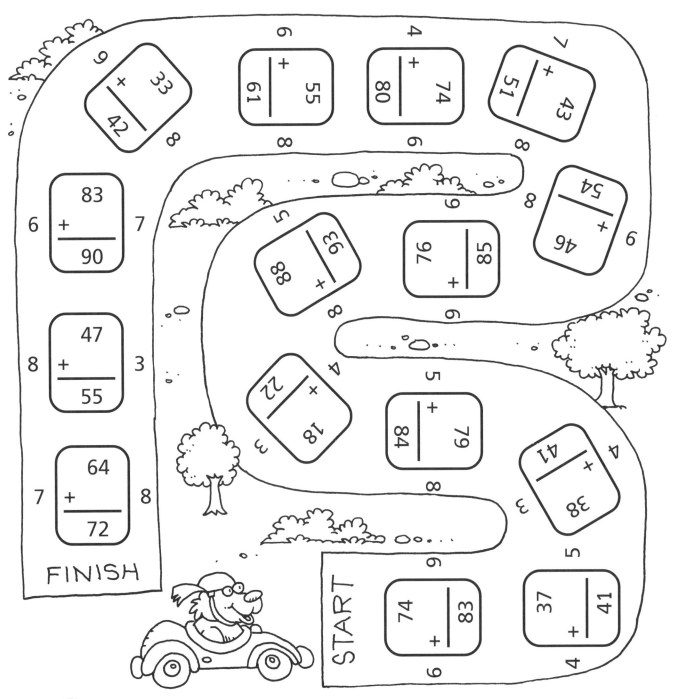

Two Letter Scramble

Two-Digit Addition Regrouping

Directions: Add. Find each pair of matching sums.
Color each pair the same color. Unscramble the letters
to make a word! Write the words at the bottom.

25 R + 16	14 S + 38	32 Y + 48	27 A + 25
18 F + 24	25 B + 15	27 O + 14	38 I + 12
39 T + 12	35 S + 15	52 M + 28	23 O + 19
16 Y + 24	36 O + 15		

Words:

_____   _____

_____   _____

_____   _____

_____

Word-Number Game

Directions: Place two game pieces at the free pick. The first player rolls a die and moves his game piece that number of spaces. The player thinks of two words that fit the category. The number of letters in each word make the two top digits in his first problem. The next player repeats this step to make the top number of her first problem. Players rolls the die again and repeat the procedure to create the bottom numbers of their problems. Each player rolls six times to make three addition problems. Add and then add the sums to find the final scores. The player with the greatest total sum wins. Note: If you can't think of a word or if your word is greater than nine letters, you get 0 points.

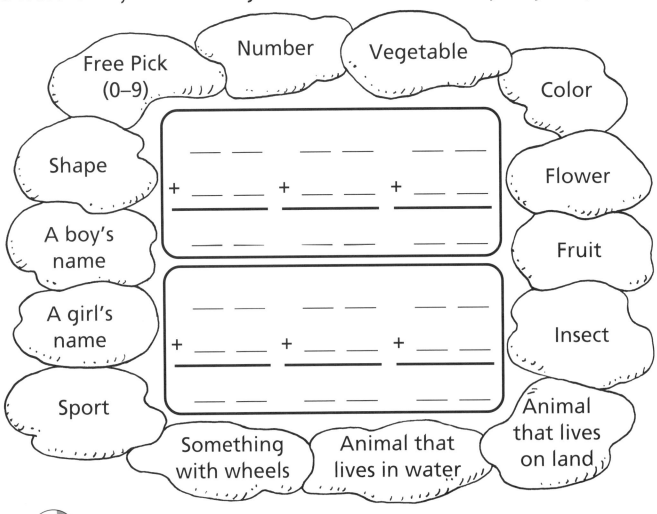

What's the Rule?

Directions: Add. Find the pattern in the sums. Write the next three numbers in the pattern along with an addition problem for each. Write the rule.

19	12	15	27		
+ 14	+ 23	+ 22	+ 12	+ ___	+ ___
33	35	37	39	41	

Rule: Add 2.

15	12	13			
+ 5	+ 11	+ 13	+ ___	+ ___	+ ___

Rule:

13	15	19			
+ 12	+ 15	+ 16	+ ___	+ ___	+ ___

Rule:

12	15	24			
+ 18	+ 25	+ 26	+ ___	+ ___	+ ___

Rule:

48	42	29			
+ 17	+ 18	+ 26	+ ___	+ ___	+ ___

Rule:

Name _____   Date _____

Message in a Bottle

Two-Digit Addition Regrouping

Directions: Add. Match the answer with each word in the key. Write the word above each problem to figure out what the message says.

[____]	[____]	[____]	[____] .	[____]
36 + 49	24 + 38	51 + 29	27 + 37	63 + 27

[____]	[____] .	[____]	[____]	[____]
48 + 23	22 + 19	57 + 24	36 + 27	45 + 46

[____] !	[____]	[____]	[____]	[____]
77 + 15	43 + 39	42 + 28	19 + 12	65 + 28

[____]	[____]	[____]	[____] .	
16 + 28	25 + 18	33 + 17	48 + 28	

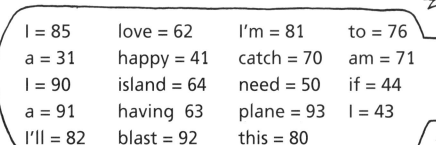

I = 85	love = 62	I'm = 81	to = 76
a = 31	happy = 41	catch = 70	am = 71
I = 90	island = 64	need = 50	if = 44
a = 91	having 63	plane = 93	I = 43
I'll = 82	blast = 92	this = 80	

Shape Code

Three-Digit Addition
No Regrouping

Directions: Use the key to rewrite each problem. Add!

1. △□○
  + ☆□△   + _____

2. ○□△
  + □○☆   + _____

3. ☆○□
  + □△○   + _____

4. ○☆□
  + □△□   + _____

5. △☆□
  + □△○   + _____

6. ○☆○
  + ○○△   + _____

7. ○◇□
  + ○○☆   + _____

8. △□○
  + ○☆□   + _____

9. ☆□○
  + ○◇□   + _____

10. ○□◇
  + ○△□   + _____

11. ☆△☆
  + □○△   + _____

12. □○○
  + △□○   + _____

Key		
1 = □	5 = ⬡	8 = ◺
2 = ○	6 = ( )	9 = ⬠
3 = △	7 = ◇	0 = ▢
4 = ☆		

Name _____ Date _____

Directions: Replace the digits that have been covered by the ink spills.

1.
```
  ⬤46
+ 2⬤
─────
 597
```

2.
```
 723
+⬤⬤
────
 854
```

3.
```
 ⬤2
+31⬤
────
 764
```

4.
```
 ⬤34
+ 5⬤
────
 758
```

5.
```
 5⬤2
+⬤8⬤
────
 698
```

6.
```
 ⬤43
+ 3⬤
────
 879
```

7.
```
 5⬤2
+16⬤
────
⬤82
```

8.
```
 ⬤43
+ 5⬤
────
 679
```

9.
```
 3⬤2
+⬤4⬤
────
 795
```

10.
```
 64⬤
+⬤2
────
 956
```

11.
```
 ⬤5⬤
+3⬤4
────
 597
```

12.
```
 2⬤
+⬤34
────
 748
```

13.
```
 ⬤2⬤
+347
────
 6⬤9
```

14.
```
 7⬤4
+⬤1⬤
────
 984
```

15.
```
 ⬤4
+35⬤
────
 595
```

Addition & Subtraction · Grades 2–3 · CD-4721

The Money Challenge

Directions: Add. Remember to include dollar signs ($) and decimal points (.). Then, take on the challenge below!

1. $5.30
    + 1.92

2. $7.42
    + 1.71

3. $4.42
    + 1.38

4. $2.18
    + 1.43

5. $1.25
    + 3.15

6. $3.72
    + 1.09

7. $2.41
    + 1.39

8. $1.21
    + 1.83

9. $3.41
    + 1.19

10. $6.84
    + 1.32

11. $1.23
    + 0.17

12. $3.45
    + 2.26

The Challenge!

A. Draw a diamond around the answer that is the greatest amount of money.

B. Draw a triangle around the answer that is the least amount of money.

C. Draw a square around all answers that are between $5.00 and $8.00.

D. Draw a circle around all answers that are less than $5.00, except for the one that is the least amount of money.

Name _____ Date _____

Rabbit's House

Directions: Take the tour. Add from room to room until you find Rabbit.

342
+ 193

632
+ 318

146
+ 291

843
+ 112

764
+ 219

641
+ 329

648
+ 191

746
+ 129

423
+ 191

389
+ 203

465
+ 182

546
+ 115

Addition & Subtraction • Grades 2–3 • CD-4721

© Carson-Dellosa

Big Numbers

Directions: Add.

1. 3,204 + 1,323	2. 5,426 + 1,231	3. 6,428 + 1,261
4. 6,412 + 1,257	5. 3,218 + 1,523	6. 6,815 + 1,423
7. 5,618 + 1,501	8. 3,245 + 3,491	9. 4,642 + 1,163
10. 6,204 + 1,347	11. 7,245 + 1,381	12. 4,985 + 2,513

Name _____ Date _____

Least to Greatest!

Two-Digit Subtraction • No Regrouping

Directions: Subtract. Place the answers in order from least to greatest.

1.

74	34	58
− 23	− 12	− 47

____ ____ ____

2.

85	74	98
− 32	− 61	− 64

____ ____ ____

3.

29	54	86
− 12	− 41	− 21

____ ____ ____

4.

76	49	84
− 21	− 13	− 21

____ ____ ____

5.

95	39	68
− 22	− 12	− 25

____ ____ ____

6.

88	48	59
− 25	− 12	− 13

____ ____ ____

Name _____ Date _____

Subtraction Downs

Two-Digit Subtraction Regrouping

Directions: Subtract. Race to the finish!

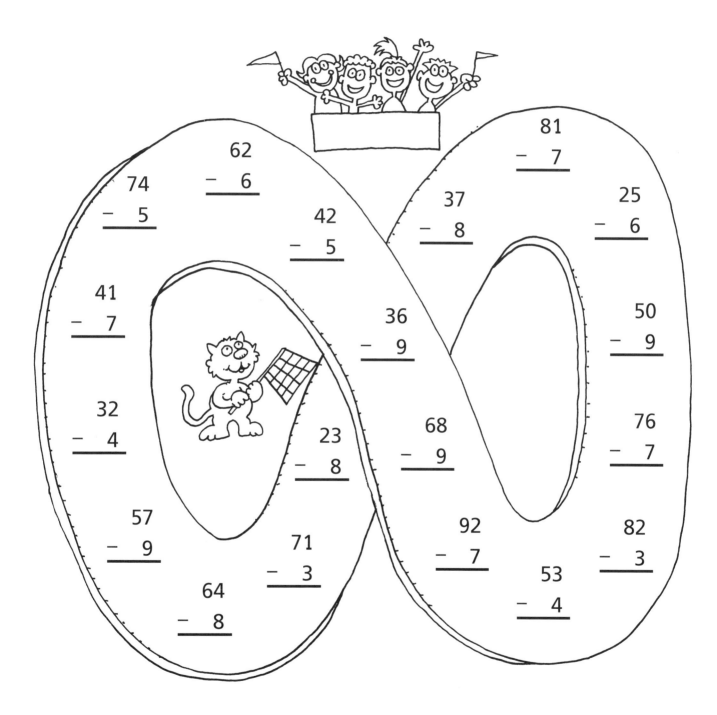

$$74 - 5$$

$$62 - 6$$

$$42 - 5$$

$$41 - 7$$

$$32 - 4$$

$$57 - 9$$

$$64 - 8$$

$$23 - 8$$

$$71 - 3$$

$$36 - 9$$

$$68 - 9$$

$$92 - 7$$

$$53 - 4$$

$$81 - 7$$

$$37 - 8$$

$$25 - 6$$

$$50 - 9$$

$$76 - 7$$

$$82 - 3$$

Jack and the Bean Stalk

Subtraction with Zero Regrouping

Directions: Subtract to climb to the top of the bean stalk.

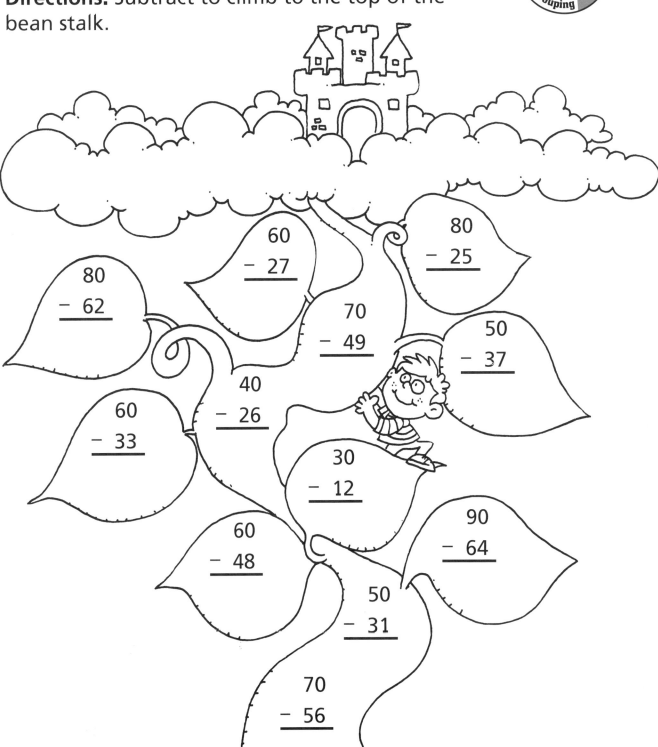

$$\begin{array}{r} 80 \\ -\ 62 \\ \hline \end{array}$$

$$\begin{array}{r} 60 \\ -\ 27 \\ \hline \end{array}$$

$$\begin{array}{r} 80 \\ -\ 25 \\ \hline \end{array}$$

$$\begin{array}{r} 70 \\ -\ 49 \\ \hline \end{array}$$

$$\begin{array}{r} 50 \\ -\ 37 \\ \hline \end{array}$$

$$\begin{array}{r} 40 \\ -\ 26 \\ \hline \end{array}$$

$$\begin{array}{r} 60 \\ -\ 33 \\ \hline \end{array}$$

$$\begin{array}{r} 30 \\ -\ 12 \\ \hline \end{array}$$

$$\begin{array}{r} 90 \\ -\ 64 \\ \hline \end{array}$$

$$\begin{array}{r} 60 \\ -\ 48 \\ \hline \end{array}$$

$$\begin{array}{r} 50 \\ -\ 31 \\ \hline \end{array}$$

$$\begin{array}{r} 70 \\ -\ 56 \\ \hline \end{array}$$

Name _____ Date _____

Directions: Subtract. Find the answers hidden in the landscape.

25   9

24

16

68

48

$$\begin{array}{r}64\\-\ 39\\\hline\end{array}$$

27

19   69

$$\begin{array}{r}71\\-\ 48\\\hline\end{array}$$ $$\begin{array}{r}92\\-\ 23\\\hline\end{array}$$

$$\begin{array}{r}34\\-\ 18\\\hline\end{array}$$ $$\begin{array}{r}52\\-\ 28\\\hline\end{array}$$ $$\begin{array}{r}83\\-\ 35\\\hline\end{array}$$

17

$$\begin{array}{r}37\\-\ 28\\\hline\end{array}$$ $$\begin{array}{r}87\\-\ 19\\\hline\end{array}$$ $$\begin{array}{r}45\\-\ 26\\\hline\end{array}$$

$$\begin{array}{r}74\\-\ 57\\\hline\end{array}$$ $$\begin{array}{r}61\\-\ 34\\\hline\end{array}$$ $$\begin{array}{r}56\\-\ 17\\\hline\end{array}$$

23

39

What a Dive!

Three-Digit Subtraction
No Regrouping

Directions: Put on your scuba gear and subtract!

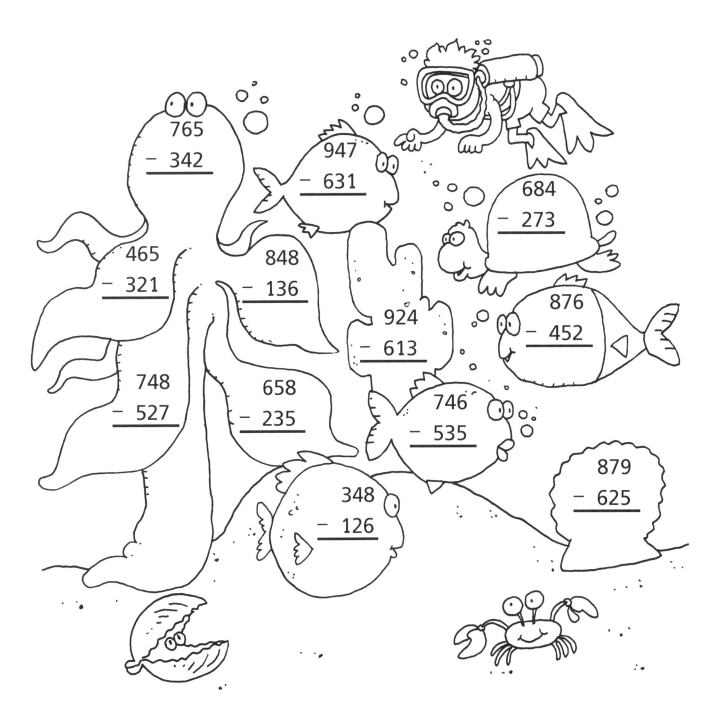

$$765 - 342$$

$$947 - 631$$

$$684 - 273$$

$$465 - 321$$

$$848 - 136$$

$$876 - 452$$

$$924 - 613$$

$$748 - 527$$

$$658 - 235$$

$$746 - 535$$

$$348 - 126$$

$$879 - 625$$

Subtraction Station

Directions: Subtract.

$$\begin{array}{r} 649 \\ -\ 562 \\ \hline \end{array}$$

$$\begin{array}{r} 783 \\ -\ 215 \\ \hline \end{array}$$

$$\begin{array}{r} 929 \\ -\ 671 \\ \hline \end{array}$$

$$\begin{array}{r} 547 \\ -\ 368 \\ \hline \end{array}$$

$$\begin{array}{r} 894 \\ -\ 397 \\ \hline \end{array}$$

$$\begin{array}{r} 942 \\ -\ 686 \\ \hline \end{array}$$

$$\begin{array}{r} 725 \\ -\ 246 \\ \hline \end{array}$$

$$\begin{array}{r} 508 \\ -\ 479 \\ \hline \end{array}$$

$$\begin{array}{r} 982 \\ -\ 694 \\ \hline \end{array}$$

$$\begin{array}{r} 532 \\ -\ 277 \\ \hline \end{array}$$

$$\begin{array}{r} 654 \\ -\ 282 \\ \hline \end{array}$$

$$\begin{array}{r} 616 \\ -\ 289 \\ \hline \end{array}$$

$$\begin{array}{r} 748 \\ -\ 259 \\ \hline \end{array}$$

$$\begin{array}{r} 719 \\ -\ 544 \\ \hline \end{array}$$

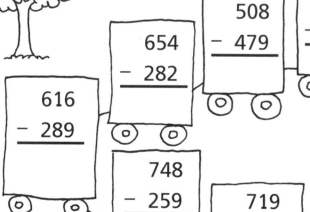

$$\begin{array}{r} 830 \\ -\ 662 \\ \hline \end{array}$$

Make the Most of It!

Directions: Write the digits 0–9 on two sets of index cards. (There will be two 0s, two 1s, etc.) Place all of the cards face down and mix them up. The first player picks three cards to make up the top number (minuend) in a subtraction problem. Three more cards are picked for the bottom number (subtrahend). The player may place each set of three cards in the order that will give him the greatest possible difference. The player then subtracts. Player two builds a subtraction problem and then subtracts. The player with the greatest difference gets a point! Players build six problems. The player with the most points, wins!

Player 1   Player 2

The Big Prediction

Directions: Circle the problem you predict will have more money in the difference. Subtract and compare. Explain how you made your predictions.

$3.42 $4.65
− 1.29   − 2.38

Were you right? _____

Explain your prediction.

_____

_____

$7.80 $5.25
− 3.24   − 3.32

Were you right? _____

Explain your prediction.

_____

_____

$8.48 $5.65
− 3.27   − 0.38

Were you right? _____

Explain your prediction.

_____

_____

$9.48 $7.37
− 6.29   − 4.52

Were you right? _____

Explain your prediction.

_____

_____

Great Numbers

Subtraction of Large Numbers • Regrouping

Directions: Subtract.

1. 6,298
    − 3,154

2. 7,278
    − 4,165

3. 8,946
    − 3,415

4. 5,468
    − 4,103

5. 8,949
    − 7,628

6. 8,143
    − 5,032

7. 9,546
    − 6,328

8. 5,643
    − 2,451

9. 8,497
    − 3,148

10. 6,485
     − 3,523

11. 8,546
     − 3,293

12. 7,846
     − 3,427

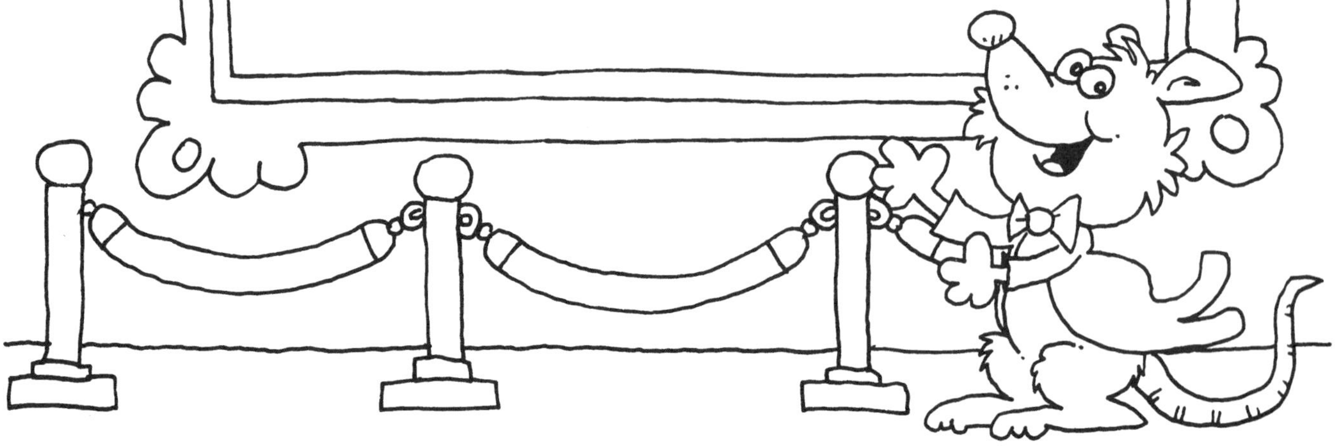

Name _____ Date _____

End-of-Book Test

Assessment
Grades 2-3

Directions: Answer the questions.

1. Add.

$$\begin{array}{c} 5 \\ +\ 3 \\ \hline \end{array} \qquad \begin{array}{c} 8 \\ +\ 9 \\ \hline \end{array} \qquad \begin{array}{c} 6 \\ +\ 2 \\ \hline \end{array} \qquad \begin{array}{c} 4 \\ +\ 0 \\ \hline \end{array}$$

2. Which is the missing addend? $3 + \underline{\quad} = 9$

  a. 7   b. 3   c. 6   d. 9

3. What does this number line show?

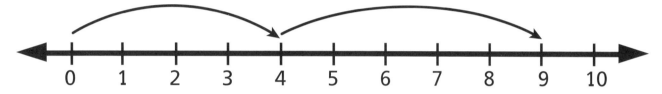

  a. $2 + 6 = 8$ b. $5 + 4 = 9$ c. $4 + 5 = 9$ d. $2 + 5 = 7$

4. Solve. Which two equations show the commutative property?

  F) $3 + 5 = 8$ G) $2 + 8 = 10$ H) $6 + 4 = 10$ J) $5 + 3 = 8$

  a. F and G   b. H and J   c. G and H   d. F and J

5. Subtract.

   $5 - 5 =$ $6 - 6 =$ $3 - 3 =$

6. Add. $(8 + 9) + 3 =$

  a. 18   b. 20   c. 15   d. 25

7. Add. $4 + (5 + 6) =$

  a. 15   b. 12   c. 17   d. 18

8. Add. $5 + 3 + 6 + 4 =$

  a. 16   b. 14   c. 18   d. 20

End-of-Book Test

9. Measure with a centimeter ruler. Add.

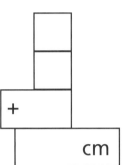

cm

   a. 12 cm   b. 14 cm   c. 20 cm   d. 18 cm

10. Compare using >, <, or =. $6 - 1 =$ ____ ☐ $9 - 8 =$ ____

11. Add.   27¢
        + 41¢

    a. 45¢   b. 68¢   c. 89¢

12. Add.   346
        + 132

    a. 274   b. 478   c. 358

13. Subtract.   568
           − 172

14. Add.   463
       + 284

15. Subtract. $9.40
           − 3.15

16. Add. $3.47
       + 1.23

17. Subtract.   5,498
           − 2,169

18. Add.   2,145
       + 1,432

Answer Key

Page 5

Shapes should be colored so that a red plus sign is visible.

$5 + 1 = 6$, $0 + 7 = 7$, $3 + 4 = 7$, $4 + 2 = 6$,
$4 + 4 = 8$, $5 + 5 = 10$, $2 + 7 = 9$, $3 + 3 = 6$,
$4 + 5 = 9$, $6 + 2 = 8$, $10 + 0 = 10$, $3 + 7 = 10$,
$8 + 0 = 8$, $5 + 3 = 8$, $6 + 4 = 10$, $8 + 1 = 9$,
$9 + 0 = 9$, $3 + 6 = 9$, $7 + 1 = 8$, $2 + 8 = 10$,
$5 + 1 = 6$, $0 + 7 = 7$, $6 + 1 = 7$, $2 + 5 = 7$

Page 6

$2 + 3 = 5$, $4 + 2 = 6$, $7 + 2 = 9$, $1 + 3 = 4$,
$3 + 3 = 6$, $2 + 4 = 6$, $2 + 5 = 7$, $1 + 2 = 3$,
$6 + 2 = 8$, $8 + 2 = 10$, $1 + 5 = 6$, $2 + 2 = 4$,
$0 + 3 = 3$, $3 + 4 = 7$

Page 7

$7 + 3 = 10$, $9 + 1 = 10$; $4 + 4 = 8$, $6 + 2 = 8$; $5 + 2 = 7$,
$3 + 4 = 7$; $4 + 1 = 5$, $3 + 2 = 5$; $5 + 4 = 9$, $7 + 2 = 9$,
$8 + 1 = 9$, $6 + 3 = 9$; $3 + 1 = 4$, $2 + 2 = 4$; $5 + 1 = 6$,
$3 + 3 = 6$

Page 8

Connect like sums: $8 + 2 = 10$, $5 + 5 = 10$, $7 + 3 = 10$,
$6 + 4 = 10$; $3 + 3 = 6$, $2 + 4 = 6$; $2 + 3 = 5$, $1 + 4 = 5$;
$4 + 5 = 9$, $6 + 3 = 9$; $2 + 5 = 7$, $3 + 4 = 7$; $7 + 5 = 12$,
$3 + 9 = 12$; $3 + 1 = 4$, $2 + 2 = 4$; $1 + 7 = 8$, $4 + 4 = 8$;
$5 + 6 = 11$, $8 + 2 = 11$

Page 9

CLIMBING HIGHER IN MATH!

Page 10

Color the following shapes yellow:
$9 + 9 = 18$, $6 + 8 = 14$, $2 + 2 = 4$, $9 + 7 = 16$,
$7 + 7 = 14$, $6 + 4 = 10$, $9 + 3 = 12$

Color the following shapes blue: $4 + 5 = 9$,
$5 + 2 = 7$, $9 + 6 = 15$, $9 + 4 = 13$, $7 + 2 = 9$, $8 + 9 = 17$,
$8 + 5 = 13$, $9 + 4 = 13$, $8 + 7 = 15$, $5 + 6 = 11$

Page 11

$4 + 5 = 9$, $5 + 4 = 9$, ladybug; $7 + 6 = 13$, $6 + 7 = 13$,
goldfish; $8 + 5 = 13$, $5 + 8 = 13$, butterfly; $9 + 8 = 17$,
$8 + 9 = 17$, ponytail; $5 + 3 = 8$, $3 + 5 = 8$, birthday;
$2 + 3 = 5$, $3 + 2 = 5$, sidewalk; $7 + 4 = 11$, $4 + 7 = 11$,
homework; $8 + 2 = 10$, $2 + 8 = 10$, sandbox; $1 + 9 = 10$,
$9 + 1 = 10$, rainbow; $9 + 4 = 13$, $4 + 9 = 13$, airplane

Page 12

$8 + 0 = 8$, $5 - 5 = 0$, $7 + 0 = 7$, $9 - 0 = 9$, $6 + 0 = 6$,
$4 - 4 = 0$, $1 + 0 = 1$

Page 13

$6 + 3 + 5 = 14$, $1 + 8 + 5 = 14$, $5 + 4 + 3 = 12$,
$5 + 4 + 6 = 15$, $2 + 5 + 7 = 14$, $3 + 7 + 4 = 14$,
$3 + 6 + 3 = 12$, $7 + 6 + 2 = 15$, $3 + 5 + 2 = 10$,
$4 + 8 + 2 = 14$, $7 + 2 + 4 = 13$, $4 + 5 + 1 = 10$,
$7 + 8 + 1 = 16$, $5 + 9 + 3 = 17$, $2 + 1 + 4 = 7$

Page 14

1. 10, 2. 12, 3. 11, 4. 13, 5. 10, 6. 17, 7. 9, 8. 14

Page 15

1. $1 + 2 + 2 + 3 = 8$, 8cm; 2. $2 + 2 + 3 = 7$, 7cm;
3. $1 + 3 + 3 + 2 = 9$, 9 cm; 4. $2 + 2 + 2 + 2 = 8$, 8cm;
5. $5 + 2 + 3 = 10$, 10 cm; 6. $2 + 3 + 6 + 3 = 14$, 14 cm;
7. $4 + 1 + 4 + 1 = 10$, 10 cm

Page 16

1. $2 + 4 + 2 + 3 = 11$cm, 2. $5 + 3 + 4 + 2 = 14$cm,
3. $2 + 7 + 3 + 6 = 18$cm, 4. $3 + 4 + 2 + 5 = 14$cm,
5. $6 + 2 + 5 + 1 = 14$cm

Page 17

blue: $10 - 6 = 4$, $5 - 1 = 4$, $6 - 2 = 4$,; green: $5 - 3$
$= 2$, $7 - 5 = 2$; yellow: $8 - 5 = 3$, $7 - 4 = 3$, $9 - 6 = 3$,
$10 - 7 = 3$; red: $9 - 4 = 5$, $8 - 3 = 5$; purple: $9 - 3$
$= 6$; orange: $4 - 3 = 1$, $3 - 2 = 1$

Page 18

Left to right and top to bottom: >, <, >, =, >, <, <, =

Page 19

Across: 2. six, 4. eight, 5. seven, 7. six, 8. three, 9. five,
10. four, 11. seven, 12. three; Down: 1. eight, 3. five,
5. six, 6. nine, 7. seven, 8. two, 9. five, 10. four

Page 20

frog #7: $13 - 6 = 7$, $12 - 5 = 7$, $14 - 7 = 7$, $14 - 8 = 6$,
$13 - 7 = 6$, $15 - 7 = 8$, $12 - 6 = 6$; frog #5: $14 - 6 = 8$,
$13 - 8 = 5$, $15 - 9 = 6$, $11 - 4 = 7$, $14 - 9 = 5$, $10 - 5 = 5$,
$15 - 8 = 7$; frog # 4: $13 - 9 = 4$, $9 - 2 = 7$, $11 - 9 = 2$,
$10 - 6 = 4$, $10 - 4 = 6$, $12 - 8 = 4$, $15 - 6 = 9$; frog #3:
$14 - 5 = 9$, $9 - 6 = 3$, $12 - 4 = 8$, $11 - 3 = 8$, $10 - 7 = 3$,
$13 - 5 = 8$, $11 - 8 = 3$; Frog #3 is the winner.

Page 21

$3 + 9 = 12$, $12 - 9 = 3$, $9 + 3 = 12$, $12 - 3 = 9$; $6 +$
$7 = 13$, $13 - 7 = 6$, $7 + 6 = 13$, $13 - 6 = 7$; $7 + 8 =$
15, $15 - 8 = 7$, $8 + 7 = 15$, $15 - 7 = 8$; $5 + 6 = 11$,
$11 - 6 = 5$, $6 + 5 = 11$, $11 - 5 = 6$; $9 + 5 = 14$, $14 -$
$5 = 9$, $5 + 9 = 14$, $14 - 9 = 5$; $7 + 9 = 16$, $16 - 9 =$
7, $9 + 7 = 16$, $16 - 7 = 9$

Page 22

1. 14, 2. 1, 3. 20, 4. 7, 5. 11

Page 23

1. >, 2. >, 3. >, 4. <, 5. <, 6. >, 7. <, 8. =, 9. =, 10. <,
11. <, 12. >, 13. >, 14. >, 15. >
Mr. Addition: 8 (winner), Mr. Subtraction: 5

Page 24

Eva: 59¢, Katelyn: 75¢ (circle); David: 79¢ (circle),
Mark: 67¢; Marlene: 49¢ (circle), Gwen: 44¢;
Earl: 78¢, Heather: 79¢ (circle); Aaron: 69¢,
Natania: 79¢ (circle); Aiko: 86¢ (circle), Cheryl:
75¢; Kanoa: 58¢ (circle), Tabitha: 57¢;
Amy: 46¢, Wolfgang: 87¢ (circle)

Answer Key

Page 25
Parts should be colored so that the words *Hi Mom* are visible. 1. 78, 2. 88, 3. 58, 4. 89, 5. 79, 6. 78, 7. 75, 8. 98, 9. 59, 10. 78, 11. 79, 12. 84, 13. 98, 14. 97, 15. 87, 16. 96, 17. 79, 18. 57, 19. 78, 20. 78

Page 26
9, 4, 3, 5, 4, 5, 9, 8, 8, 6, 6, 9, 7, 8, 8

Page 27
25 + 16 = 41 and 27 + 14 = 41, OR; 14 + 38 = 52 and 27 + 25 = 52, AS; 32 + 48 = 80 and 52 + 28 = 80, MY; 18 + 24 = 42 and 23 + 19 = 42, OF; 25 + 15 = 40 and 16 + 24 = 40, BY; 39 + 12 = 51 and 36 + 15 = 57, TO; 38 + 12 = 50 and 35 + 15 = 50, IS

Page 29
Row 1: 39, 41, 43; Row 2: 20, 22, 26, 29, 32, 35 (add 3); Row 3: 25, 30, 35, 40, 45, 50 (add 5); Row 4: 30, 40, 50, 60, 70, 80 (add 10); Row 5: 65, 60, 55, 50, 45, 40 (subtract 5); problems will vary

Page 30
I love this island. I am happy. I'm having a blast! I'll catch a plane if I need to.

Page 31
1. 312 + 413 = 725, 2. 613 + 124 = 737,
3. 420 + 132 = 552, 4. 241 + 131 = 372,
5. 341 + 132 = 473, 6. 546 + 253 = 799,
7. 271 + 524 = 795, 8. 316 + 241 = 557,
9. 415 + 270 = 685, 10. 207 + 281 = 488,
11. 434 + 123 = 557, 12. 165 + 302 = 467

Page 32
1. 346 + 251 = 597, 2. 723 + 131 = 854, 3. 452 + 312 = 764, 4. 234 + 524 = 758, 5. 512 + 186 = 698, 6. 543 + 336 = 879, 7. 522 + 160 = 682, 8. 143 + 536 = 679, 9. 352 + 443 = 795, 10. 644 + 312 = 956, 11. 253 + 344 = 597, 12. 214 + 534 = 748, 13. 322 + 347 = 669, 14. 774 + 210 = 984, 15. 244 + 351 = 595

Page 33
1. $7.22 (square), 2. $9.13 (diamond),
3. $5.80 (square), 4. $3.61 (circle), 5. $4.40 (circle), 6. $4.81 (circle), 7. $3.80 (circle), 8. $3.04 (circle), 9. $4.60 (circle), 10. $8.16, 11. $1.40 (triangle), 12. $5.71 (square)

Page 34
342 + 193 = 535, 632 + 318 = 950,
146 + 291 = 437, 641 + 329 = 970,
843 + 112 = 955, 764 + 219 = 983,
648 + 191 = 839, 746 + 129 = 875,
423 + 191 = 614, 465 + 182 = 647,
389 + 203 = 592, 546 + 115 = 661

Page 35
1. 4,527; 2. 6,657; 3. 7,689; 4. 7,669;
5. 4,741; 6. 8,238; 7. 7,119; 8. 6,736;
9. 5,805; 10. 7,551; 11. 8,626; 12. 7,498

Page 36
1. 51, 22, 11—11, 22, 51; 2. 53, 13, 34—13, 34, 53; 3. 17, 13, 65—13, 17, 65; 4. 55, 36, 63—36, 55, 63; 5. 73, 27, 43—27, 43, 73; 6. 63, 36, 46—36, 46, 63

Page 37
Starting at 37 – 8, following the track to the right and ending at 23 – 8: 29, 74, 19, 41, 69, 79, 49, 85, 57, 27, 37, 54, 69, 34, 28, 48, 56, 68, 15

Page 38
80 – 62 = 18, 60 – 27 = 32, 80 – 25 = 55,
60 – 33 = 27, 40 – 26 = 14, 70 – 49 = 21,
50 – 37 = 13, 60 – 48 = 12, 30 – 12 = 18,
50 – 37 = 13, 70 – 56 = 14, 50 – 31 = 29,
90 – 64 = 26

Page 39
Left to right and top to bottom: 25, 23, 69, 16, 24, 48, 9, 68, 19, 17, 27, 39

Page 40
765 – 342 = 423, 947 – 631 = 316, 684 – 273 = 411, 465 – 321 = 144, 848 – 136 = 712, 924 – 613 = 311, 876 – 452 = 424, 748 – 527 = 221, 658 – 235 = 423, 746 – 535 = 211, 348 – 126 = 222, 879 – 625 = 254

Page 41
Following the train from rear to engine: 87, 568, 258, 179, 497, 260, 479, 255, 288, 29, 372, 327, 489, 175, 168

Page 43
$2.13, $2.27; $4.56, $1.93; 3. $5.21, $5.27; $3.19, $2.85

Page 44
1. 3,144; 2. 3,113; 3. 5,531; 4. 1,365; 5. 1,321;
6. 3,111; 7. 3,218; 8. 3,192; 9. 5,349; 10. 2,962;
11. 5,253; 12. 4,419

Page 45
1. 8, 17, 8, 4; 2. C; 3. C; 4. D.; 5. 0, 0, 0; 6. B; 7. A; 8. C;

Page 46
9. 5 + 2 + 7 = 14cm, B.;10. 6 – 1 = 5 > 9 – 8 = 1; 11. B.; 12. B.; 13. 396; 14. 747; 15. $6.25; 16. $4.70; 17. 3,319; 18. 3,577